Table of Contents

Chapter 1: Introduction to Personalized AI

Overview of Personalized AI

The subchapter "Overview of Personalized AI" provides a comprehensive look at how artificial intelligence is transforming user experiences across various industries. From entertainment to ecommerce, AI is driving highly personalized interactions by leveraging sophisticated recommendation algorithms to tailor content and services to individual preferences. This approach not only enhances user engagement but also boosts satisfaction, ultimately leading to increased loyalty and retention.

In the realm of healthcare, AI is revolutionizing personalized medicine by tailoring medical treatments and healthcare services to individual patient needs and preferences. By analyzing vast amounts of data, AI can identify patterns and trends that help healthcare providers deliver more effective and targeted care. This personalized approach not only improves patient outcomes but also reduces costs and enhances overall healthcare quality.

In the field of education, AI is being used to create personalized learning experiences for students based on their unique learning styles and abilities. By leveraging AI technology, educators can customize lesson plans, assignments, and assessments to meet the individual needs of each student, ultimately improving learning outcomes and driving student success.

In finance, AI algorithms are being employed to offer personalized financial advice and solutions to individuals based on their financial goals and habits. By analyzing spending patterns, investment preferences, and risk tolerance levels, AI can provide tailored recommendations that help individuals achieve their financial objectives and secure their financial future.

Across various sectors such as travel, fitness, fashion, marketing, gaming, home automation, and customer service, AI is playing a crucial role in delivering personalized experiences that cater to individual preferences and behaviors. By harnessing the power of AI, organizations can create more engaging, efficient, and satisfying interactions that drive customer loyalty and business growth. This subchapter serves as a foundational guide for professionals looking to explore the vast potential of AI for personalization in their respective industries.

Importance of AI in Personalization

The importance of AI in personalization cannot be overstated, as it is revolutionizing user experiences across various industries. From entertainment to ecommerce, AI is driving highly personalized interactions by utilizing sophisticated recommendation algorithms to tailor content and services to individual preferences. This level of personalization enhances user engagement and satisfaction, ultimately leading to increased customer loyalty and retention.

In the healthcare sector, AI is being used to personalize medical treatments and healthcare services to individual patient needs and preferences. By analyzing vast amounts of data and leveraging machine learning algorithms, healthcare providers can offer tailored solutions that improve patient outcomes and satisfaction. This personalized approach to healthcare not only enhances the overall patient experience but also leads to more efficient and effective treatment plans.

Similarly, in the education sector, AI technology is being implemented to create personalized learning experiences for students based on their unique learning styles and abilities. By analyzing student data and behavior, AI algorithms can deliver customized educational content and resources that cater to individual needs, ultimately improving student engagement and academic performance. This personalized approach to education is transforming traditional teaching methods and revolutionizing the way students learn and interact with educational material.

In the finance industry, AI algorithms are being utilized to offer personalized financial advice and solutions to individuals based on their financial goals and habits. By analyzing financial data and patterns, AI technology can provide tailored recommendations that help individuals make informed decisions about their finances. This level of personalization not only improves financial literacy but also helps individuals achieve their financial goals more effectively.

Overall, the importance of AI in personalization cannot be ignored, as it is reshaping user experiences in various sectors and driving innovation across industries. By leveraging AI technology to create highly personalized interactions, businesses can enhance customer satisfaction, improve outcomes, and drive growth in today's competitive market landscape. Professionals looking to learn more about AI for personalization should explore the diverse applications and benefits of AI technology in delivering personalized experiences across industries.

Benefits of Personalized User Experiences

The benefits of personalized user experiences in various industries are vast and impactful. By leveraging AI technology to create tailored content and services based on individual preferences, businesses can significantly enhance user engagement and satisfaction. This level of personalization not only improves the overall user experience but also increases customer loyalty and retention rates. In an age where consumers expect personalized interactions, implementing AI for personalization is crucial for staying competitive in the market.

One of the key benefits of personalized user experiences is in the healthcare sector. AI can be used to customize medical treatments and healthcare services to meet the specific needs and preferences of individual patients. This not only improves the quality of care but also enhances patient outcomes and satisfaction. By leveraging AI for personalization in healthcare, professionals can deliver more efficient and effective care that is tailored to each patient's unique circumstances.

In the education sector, personalized user experiences are revolutionizing the way students learn and engage with educational content. AI technology can analyze students' learning styles and abilities to create personalized learning experiences that cater to their individual needs. This not only improves academic performance but also increases student motivation and engagement. By implementing AI for personalized education, educators can create more effective teaching strategies that meet the diverse needs of students.

In the finance industry, personalized user experiences are transforming the way individuals manage their finances and achieve their financial goals. AI algorithms can analyze individuals' financial habits and goals to offer personalized financial advice and solutions. This level of personalization not only helps individuals make better financial decisions but also improves their overall financial well-being. By leveraging AI for personalized finance, financial institutions can provide more tailored services that meet the unique needs of their clients.

Overall, the benefits of personalized user experiences across various industries are profound. By leveraging AI technology to create tailored experiences based on individual preferences, businesses can improve user engagement, satisfaction, and loyalty. Whether it's in healthcare, education, finance, or any other sector, personalized user experiences are revolutionizing the way businesses interact with their customers and clients. For professionals looking to enhance user experiences through AI for personalization, understanding the benefits and implications of this technology is essential for success in today's competitive market.

Chapter 2: AI for Personalization Across Industries

AI in Entertainment

AI is revolutionizing the entertainment industry by enhancing user experiences through personalized content and services. From streaming platforms to gaming, AI-powered recommendation algorithms are being utilized to tailor entertainment options to individual preferences, increasing user engagement and satisfaction. By analyzing user behavior and preferences, AI can suggest movies, TV shows, music, and games that are likely to resonate with each user, creating a more immersive and enjoyable entertainment experience.

In the realm of streaming services, AI is being used to recommend personalized content based on viewing history, genre preferences, and user feedback. Platforms like Netflix and Spotify use sophisticated algorithms to analyze user data and provide highly customized recommendations, keeping users engaged and coming back for more. By personalizing content suggestions, these platforms are able to cater to each user's unique tastes and preferences, ultimately leading to increased user satisfaction and loyalty.

In the gaming industry, AI is being leveraged to create personalized gaming experiences that adapt to individual player preferences and skills. Game developers are using AI algorithms to customize gameplay, challenges, and rewards based on each player's gaming habits and performance. By tailoring the gaming experience to the individual player, AI is able to create a more immersive and engaging experience that keeps players coming back for more.

Furthermore, AI is also being used in the entertainment industry to personalize marketing campaigns and messages to target audiences. By analyzing user behavior and preferences, AI can tailor marketing efforts to each individual, increasing the likelihood of engagement and conversion. Whether it's promoting a new movie release or a concert tour, AI-powered marketing campaigns can deliver personalized messages that resonate with each recipient, ultimately driving higher levels of engagement and ROI.

Overall, AI is playing a crucial role in enhancing user experiences in the entertainment industry by personalizing content, services, and marketing efforts. By leveraging AI algorithms to analyze user data and preferences, entertainment companies are able to create highly customized experiences that keep users engaged and satisfied. As AI technology continues to advance, we can expect to see even more innovative applications of AI in entertainment, further enhancing the way we consume and interact with entertainment content.

AI in Ecommerce

AI in ecommerce is revolutionizing the way businesses interact with their customers. With the help of sophisticated recommendation algorithms, companies are able to tailor their products and services to individual preferences, ultimately enhancing user engagement and satisfaction. From personalized product recommendations to targeted marketing campaigns, AI is driving highly personalized user experiences in the world of online retail.

One of the key benefits of AI in ecommerce is its ability to analyze customer data in real-time, allowing businesses to better understand their customers and anticipate their needs. By leveraging machine learning algorithms, companies can create personalized shopping experiences that cater to each individual shopper's unique preferences and behaviors. This level of personalization not only increases customer loyalty but also drives higher conversion rates and sales.

In addition to personalized product recommendations, AI is also being used in ecommerce to streamline the shopping experience. Chatbots and virtual assistants powered by AI technology are now being used to provide personalized customer support and assistance, helping shoppers find the products they are looking for and answer any questions they may have. This level of personalized customer service not only enhances the overall shopping experience but also helps businesses build stronger relationships with their customers.

Furthermore, AI in ecommerce is also being used to optimize pricing strategies and inventory management. By analyzing pricing data and consumer behavior, companies can dynamically adjust prices in real-time to maximize profits and minimize stockouts. This level of automation and optimization not only improves operational efficiency but also ensures that customers are always presented with the best possible deals.

Overall, AI in ecommerce is transforming the way businesses interact with their customers, offering highly personalized shopping experiences that cater to individual preferences and needs. From personalized product recommendations to targeted marketing campaigns, AI is helping businesses drive engagement, loyalty, and sales in the highly competitive world of online retail. For professionals looking to learn more about AI for personalization, understanding how AI is being used in ecommerce is crucial for staying ahead in the rapidly evolving digital landscape.

AI in Healthcare

AI in healthcare is revolutionizing the way medical treatments and healthcare services are personalized to meet individual patient needs and preferences. By utilizing AI technology, healthcare professionals are able to analyze vast amounts of data to tailor treatments and interventions based on a patient's unique medical history, genetic makeup, and lifestyle factors. This personalized approach not only improves patient outcomes but also enhances the overall efficiency and effectiveness of healthcare delivery.

One of the key advantages of AI in healthcare is its ability to provide real-time insights and predictions that can help healthcare providers make more informed decisions. For example, AI-powered algorithms can analyze patient data to identify patterns and trends that may indicate potential health risks or predict the likelihood of certain medical conditions developing. This proactive approach to healthcare allows for early intervention and preventive measures, ultimately leading to better health outcomes for patients.

AI in healthcare is also transforming the way medical research and clinical trials are conducted. By leveraging AI algorithms, researchers are able to analyze large datasets to identify potential drug targets, predict treatment outcomes, and optimize clinical trial designs. This not only accelerates the pace of medical innovation but also allows for more personalized and targeted therapies to be developed for individual patients.

Furthermore, AI in healthcare is enhancing the patient experience by providing personalized and more accessible healthcare services. Virtual health assistants powered by AI technology can offer personalized medical advice, schedule appointments, and provide remote monitoring and support for patients with chronic conditions. This not only improves patient engagement and satisfaction but also reduces the burden on healthcare resources and facilities.

Overall, AI in healthcare is transforming the way healthcare is delivered and personalized to meet the unique needs and preferences of individual patients. By harnessing the power of AI technology, healthcare professionals are able to provide more efficient, effective, and personalized care that ultimately improves patient outcomes and enhances the overall healthcare experience.

AI in Education

AI technology is revolutionizing the field of education by enabling personalized learning experiences for students. By leveraging AI algorithms, educators can tailor educational content and teaching methods to match the unique learning styles and abilities of individual students. This not only enhances student engagement and satisfaction but also improves learning outcomes. With AI in education, students can receive personalized feedback, recommendations, and support to help them reach their full potential.

One of the key benefits of AI in education is its ability to adapt to the diverse needs and preferences of students. By analyzing data on student performance, behavior, and preferences, AI systems can create customized learning pathways for each student. This means that students can learn at their own pace, focus on areas where they need extra help, and explore topics that interest them the most. This personalized approach to education is particularly beneficial for students with different learning abilities and backgrounds.

Furthermore, AI technology in education can help educators identify and address learning gaps more effectively. By analyzing data on student performance and progress, AI systems can pinpoint areas where students are struggling and provide targeted interventions to help them improve. This can lead to more efficient and effective teaching strategies, ultimately helping students achieve better academic outcomes. In addition, AI can assist educators in creating personalized assessments and learning materials that are tailored to each student's specific needs.

Another advantage of AI in education is its potential to enhance collaboration and communication among students and teachers. AI-powered tools can facilitate peer-to-peer learning, group projects, and online discussions, enabling students to connect with their peers and teachers in new and meaningful ways. This can foster a more interactive and engaging learning environment, where students can share ideas, collaborate on projects, and receive feedback from their peers and teachers in real-time. Overall, AI technology has the potential to transform the way education is delivered and experienced, making learning more personalized, engaging, and effective for students.

In conclusion, AI technology is playing a crucial role in shaping the future of education by providing personalized learning experiences for students. By leveraging AI algorithms and data analytics, educators can create customized learning pathways, identify learning gaps, and facilitate collaboration among students and teachers. With AI in education, students can receive tailored support, feedback, and resources to help them succeed academically. As AI continues to evolve and improve, the possibilities for personalized education are endless, offering new opportunities for students to learn, grow, and thrive in the digital age.

AI in Finance

AI in Finance is revolutionizing the way individuals manage their money and make financial decisions. By utilizing AI algorithms, financial institutions are able to offer personalized financial advice and solutions to individuals based on their unique financial goals and habits. This level of personalization allows for more tailored and effective financial planning, helping individuals to achieve their financial objectives more efficiently.

One of the key advantages of AI in Finance is the ability to analyze vast amounts of data in real-time to provide personalized recommendations. By analyzing an individual's spending habits, investment preferences, and financial goals, AI algorithms can offer personalized investment advice, savings strategies, and budgeting tips. This level of personalization ensures that individuals receive financial advice that is tailored to their specific needs, leading to better financial outcomes.

AI in Finance also plays a crucial role in detecting and preventing fraud. By analyzing patterns and anomalies in financial transactions, AI algorithms are able to identify potentially fraudulent activities and alert individuals and financial institutions in real-time. This proactive approach to fraud detection helps to safeguard individuals' financial assets and prevent costly security breaches.

Furthermore, AI in Finance is reshaping the way individuals interact with financial institutions. Chatbots and virtual assistants powered by AI technology are being used to provide personalized customer support and assistance, making it easier for individuals to manage their finances and access important financial information. This level of personalized customer service enhances the overall user experience and strengthens the relationship between individuals and financial institutions.

Overall, AI in Finance is transforming the financial industry by offering personalized financial advice, detecting fraud, and enhancing customer service. As AI technology continues to advance, the level of personalization in finance will only increase, leading to more efficient and effective financial management for individuals. Professionals in the finance industry can benefit greatly from understanding and leveraging AI technology in order to provide personalized financial solutions to their clients.

AI in Travel

In the realm of personalized AI, one of the most exciting applications is in the travel industry. AI is revolutionizing the way people plan, book, and experience their trips by offering highly tailored recommendations and solutions. By leveraging sophisticated algorithms, travel companies are able to provide personalized travel itineraries, accommodations, and activities based on individual preferences. This not only enhances the overall travel experience but also increases user engagement and satisfaction.

With AI for personalized travel, users can receive recommendations that are specifically curated to match their unique interests and preferences. Whether it's suggesting the best local restaurants, must-see attractions, or hidden gems off the beaten path, AI algorithms are able to analyze vast amounts of data to provide personalized recommendations that cater to individual tastes. This level of customization allows travelers to have a truly unique and unforgettable experience that is tailored to their preferences.

Furthermore, AI in travel can also streamline the booking process by offering personalized suggestions for flights, hotels, and transportation options. By analyzing past booking behaviors and preferences, AI algorithms can predict and recommend the best travel options for each individual user. This not only saves time for travelers but also ensures that they are getting the most suitable and cost-effective options for their trip.

Additionally, AI for personalized travel can enhance the overall customer service experience by providing personalized assistance and support throughout the travel journey. Whether it's through AI-powered chatbots or virtual assistants, travelers can receive real-time recommendations, updates, and assistance tailored to their specific needs and preferences. This level of personalized customer service helps to build trust and loyalty among travelers, leading to increased satisfaction and repeat business for travel companies.

Overall, AI in travel is transforming the way people plan and experience their trips by offering highly personalized recommendations and solutions. By leveraging sophisticated algorithms and data analysis, travel companies are able to create tailored experiences that cater to individual preferences and interests. From personalized itineraries to streamlined booking processes and enhanced customer service, AI is revolutionizing the travel industry and providing users with unforgettable and unique travel experiences.

AI in Fitness

AI in fitness is revolutionizing the way individuals approach their health and wellness goals. By leveraging AI technology, personalized workout plans, nutrition advice, and fitness tracking are now more accessible than ever before. Whether someone is looking to lose weight, build muscle, or improve their overall health, AI can provide tailored recommendations to help them reach their specific goals.

One of the key benefits of AI in fitness is its ability to adapt to individual health and fitness preferences. Through advanced algorithms, AI can analyze data such as exercise performance, dietary habits, and biometric information to create customized fitness plans that are tailored to each individual's needs. This level of personalization not only improves the effectiveness of a workout routine but also enhances motivation and engagement, leading to better long-term results.

In addition to personalized workout plans, AI in fitness also offers nutrition advice based on individual dietary preferences and goals. By analyzing factors such as calorie intake, macronutrient balance, and food preferences, AI can provide recommendations for meal planning and dietary adjustments that align with an individual's health and fitness objectives. This level of personalized guidance can help individuals make informed choices about their nutrition and optimize their overall wellness.

Furthermore, AI technology in fitness enables precise tracking of progress and performance, allowing individuals to monitor their results in real-time and make adjustments as needed. By collecting and analyzing data on factors such as workout intensity, calorie burn, and sleep quality, AI can provide insights into areas for improvement and help individuals stay on track towards their fitness goals. This level of personalized feedback empowers individuals to make informed decisions about their health and wellness journey.

Overall, AI in fitness is transforming the way individuals approach their fitness routines by providing personalized guidance, motivation, and tracking tools. With the help of AI technology, individuals can optimize their workouts, nutrition plans, and overall wellness strategies to achieve their health and fitness goals more efficiently and effectively. As the fitness industry continues to evolve, AI will play a crucial role in empowering individuals to take control of their health and well-being in a personalized and sustainable way.

AI in Fashion

AI in fashion is revolutionizing the way consumers interact with brands and make purchasing decisions. By leveraging AI algorithms, fashion retailers can offer personalized recommendations and styling advice tailored to individual tastes and preferences. This level of personalization not only enhances the shopping experience for customers but also increases engagement and satisfaction, ultimately driving sales and loyalty.

One of the key benefits of AI in fashion is the ability to analyze vast amounts of data to identify trends and predict future consumer preferences. By understanding each customer's unique style, size, and preferences, retailers can offer customized product recommendations that are more likely to resonate with the individual. This level of personalization not only improves the efficiency of the shopping experience but also helps reduce returns and increase customer retention.

In addition to personalized recommendations, AI in fashion is also being used to enhance the design and manufacturing processes. By analyzing data on consumer preferences and trends, designers can create collections that are more likely to resonate with their target audience. This not only reduces the risk of producing unsold inventory but also ensures that brands are staying ahead of the curve in terms of style and innovation.

Furthermore, AI technology is being used to improve the sustainability of the fashion industry. By optimizing the supply chain and production processes, brands can reduce waste and minimize their environmental impact. AI algorithms can also help brands better understand consumer preferences for sustainable and ethically produced products, allowing them to make more informed decisions about their sourcing and manufacturing practices.

Overall, AI in fashion is transforming the industry by offering personalized experiences that cater to the unique tastes and preferences of each individual consumer. By leveraging AI algorithms to analyze data, offer recommendations, and improve sustainability practices, fashion brands can create a more engaging, efficient, and environmentally conscious shopping experience for their customers.

AI in Marketing

AI is revolutionizing the marketing industry by enabling highly personalized user experiences across various sectors. From entertainment to ecommerce, AI-driven recommendation algorithms are being utilized to tailor content and services to individual preferences. This level of personalization not only enhances user engagement but also boosts satisfaction and loyalty.

In the realm of healthcare, AI is being leveraged to provide personalized medical treatments and healthcare services to individual patient needs and preferences. By analyzing vast amounts of data, AI algorithms can recommend the most effective treatments and care plans tailored to each patient's unique health requirements.

In education, AI technology is being implemented to create personalized learning experiences for students based on their individual learning styles and abilities. By adapting teaching methods and content to meet the needs of each student, AI is transforming the way education is delivered and enhancing student outcomes.

AI is also making waves in the finance industry by offering personalized financial advice and solutions to individuals based on their financial goals and habits. By analyzing spending patterns and investment preferences, AI algorithms can provide tailored recommendations to help individuals achieve their financial objectives.

In the realm of marketing, AI is being used to deliver personalized marketing campaigns and messages to target audiences based on their preferences and behavior. By analyzing customer data and behavior, AI can identify the most effective marketing strategies to engage customers and drive conversions.AI for Personalization: AI is driving highly personalized user experiences in various sectors, from entertainment to ecommerce. Sophisticated recommendation algorithms are being used to tailor content and services to individual preferences, enhancing user engagement and satisfaction. AI for Personalized Healthcare: Using AI to tailor medical treatments and healthcare services to individual patient needs and preferences. AI for Personalized Education: Implementing AI technology to create personalized learning experiences for students based on their unique learning styles and abilities. AI for Personalized Finance: Utilizing AI algorithms to offer personalized financial advice and solutions to individuals based on their financial goals and habits. AI for Personalized Travel: Enhancing the travel experience by using AI to recommend personalized travel itineraries, accommodations, and activities based on individual preferences. AI for Personalized Fitness: Leveraging AI technology to provide personalized workout plans, nutrition advice, and fitness tracking based on individual health and fitness goals. AI for Personalized Fashion: Using AI algorithms to offer personalized fashion recommendations and styling advice tailored to individual tastes and preferences. AI for Personalized Marketing: Implementing AI technology to deliver personalized marketing campaigns and messages to target audiences based on their preferences and behavior. AI for Personalized Gaming: Enhancing the gaming experience by using AI to customize gameplay, challenges, and rewards based on individual player preferences and skills. AI for Personalized Home Automation: Using AI technology to create personalized smart home experiences that adapt to individual preferences for lighting, temperature, security, and entertainment. AI for Personalized Customer Service: Utilizing AI-powered chatbots and virtual assistants to provide personalized customer support and assistance based on individual needs and preferences.

AI in Gaming

AI in gaming is revolutionizing the way players experience their favorite games. From customizing gameplay to providing tailored challenges and rewards, AI is enhancing the gaming experience for players of all skill levels. By analyzing player preferences and skills, AI algorithms can create personalized gaming experiences that keep players engaged and satisfied.

One of the key ways AI is being used in gaming is through adaptive difficulty levels. Instead of having a one-size-fits-all approach to gameplay, AI can adjust the difficulty of a game based on the player's skill level and progress. This ensures that players are constantly challenged without feeling frustrated or overwhelmed. By dynamically adjusting the level of difficulty, AI keeps players motivated and invested in the game.

Another way AI is enhancing the gaming experience is through personalized recommendations. Just like how AI algorithms recommend movies or products based on individual preferences, AI in gaming can suggest new games, levels, or in-game items that align with a player's interests and playing style. This not only helps players discover new content but also keeps them engaged and excited to continue playing.

AI in gaming is also being used to create personalized virtual assistants within games. These AI-powered characters can provide players with hints, tips, and strategies tailored to their specific needs. Whether it's helping a player navigate a challenging level or suggesting the best weapon for a particular enemy, AI assistants enhance the gaming experience by providing personalized support and guidance.

Overall, AI in gaming is transforming the way players interact with their favorite games. By customizing gameplay, challenges, and rewards based on individual preferences and skills, AI is creating highly personalized gaming experiences that keep players engaged and satisfied. As the technology continues to advance, we can expect even more innovative uses of AI in gaming to enhance the player experience.

AI in Home Automation

AI technology is revolutionizing the way we interact with our homes, creating personalized smart home experiences that adapt to individual preferences for lighting, temperature, security, and entertainment. Through the use of sophisticated algorithms, AI-powered devices can learn user habits and preferences to automate and optimize various aspects of home living.

Imagine coming home to a house that knows exactly how you like your lighting and temperature settings. With AI in home automation, smart devices can adjust these settings automatically based on your daily routines and personal preferences, creating a comfortable and welcoming environment tailored just for you.

AI-powered security systems can also enhance home safety by analyzing patterns and behaviors to detect and prevent potential threats. From monitoring activity around the house to identifying unfamiliar faces, these intelligent systems provide an extra layer of protection for homeowners, giving them peace of mind and a sense of security.

Furthermore, AI in home automation can elevate the entertainment experience within the home. By analyzing viewing habits and preferences, smart devices can recommend personalized content and suggest new shows or movies that align with individual tastes, creating a more engaging and enjoyable entertainment experience for users.

Overall, AI in home automation is transforming the way we interact with our living spaces, making them more intelligent, intuitive, and personalized. For professionals looking to enhance user experiences in the realm of home automation, understanding and implementing AI technology is essential to creating smart homes that cater to individual needs and preferences.

AI in Customer Service

AI in customer service is revolutionizing the way businesses interact with their customers. By incorporating artificial intelligence into customer support processes, companies are able to provide personalized and efficient service to each individual customer. AI-powered chatbots and virtual assistants are being used to answer customer queries, provide product recommendations, and even handle transactions seamlessly. This level of customization not only enhances user satisfaction but also increases customer loyalty and retention rates.

One of the key benefits of AI in customer service is the ability to provide round-the-clock support. With AI-powered chatbots, businesses can offer 24/7 assistance to customers, regardless of time zones or geographical locations. This ensures that customers are able to receive help whenever they need it, leading to faster issue resolution and improved overall customer experience. Additionally, AI allows for quick and accurate responses to customer inquiries, reducing the need for customers to wait in long queues or speak to multiple agents before getting the help they need.

Furthermore, AI in customer service enables businesses to gather valuable insights about their customers' preferences and behavior. By analyzing customer interactions with chatbots and virtual assistants, companies can gain a better understanding of what their customers are looking for and tailor their products and services accordingly. This level of personalization not only improves the customer experience but also helps businesses to increase sales and drive revenue growth.

Another advantage of AI in customer service is the ability to handle a large volume of customer inquiries simultaneously. Unlike human agents who can only handle a limited number of conversations at a time, AI-powered chatbots can engage with multiple customers simultaneously, providing quick and efficient responses to each individual. This not only improves response times but also ensures that no customer is left waiting for assistance, leading to higher levels of customer satisfaction and retention.

In conclusion, AI in customer service is a powerful tool that can help businesses deliver personalized and efficient support to their customers. By leveraging AI-powered chatbots and virtual assistants, companies can offer round-the-clock assistance, gather valuable customer insights, handle a large volume of inquiries simultaneously, and ultimately enhance the overall customer experience. For professionals looking to enhance their customer service strategies, incorporating AI into their processes is a key step towards achieving success in today's competitive market.

Chapter 3: Implementing AI for Personalization

Understanding User Preferences

Understanding user preferences is essential in the world of personalized AI, where algorithms are used to tailor content and services to individual needs and preferences. In various sectors, from entertainment to ecommerce, AI is driving highly personalized user experiences. By analyzing user data and behavior, sophisticated recommendation algorithms can enhance user engagement and satisfaction by offering relevant and personalized recommendations.

In the realm of personalized healthcare, AI is revolutionizing the way medical treatments and healthcare services are delivered. By leveraging AI technology, healthcare providers can tailor treatments to individual patient needs and preferences, leading to more effective and personalized care. From personalized medication dosages to treatment plans, AI is helping to improve patient outcomes and overall healthcare experiences.

In the field of personalized education, AI is being used to create customized learning experiences for students based on their unique learning styles and abilities. By analyzing student data and behavior, AI algorithms can recommend personalized learning materials, assignments, and assessments, ultimately improving student engagement and academic performance. Personalized education powered by AI is transforming traditional teaching methods and enhancing the learning experience for students of all ages.

In personalized finance, AI algorithms are utilized to offer personalized financial advice and solutions to individuals based on their financial goals and habits. By analyzing financial data and behavior, AI can provide tailored recommendations for budgeting, investing, and saving, helping individuals make more informed financial decisions. Personalized finance powered by AI is revolutionizing the way individuals manage their money and plan for their financial future.

In personalized travel, AI is enhancing the travel experience by recommending personalized travel itineraries, accommodations, and activities based on individual preferences. By analyzing travel data and behavior, AI algorithms can create customized travel plans that cater to each traveler's unique preferences and interests. Personalized travel experiences powered by AI are transforming the way people plan and enjoy their vacations, making travel more convenient, enjoyable, and memorable.

Developing Recommendation Algorithms

In the subchapter "Developing Recommendation Algorithms" of the book "Personalized AI: Enhancing User Experiences Across Industries," we dive deep into the intricate process of creating sophisticated recommendation algorithms that drive highly personalized user experiences. These algorithms are at the forefront of AI technology, shaping the way content and services are tailored to individual preferences across various sectors, from entertainment to ecommerce. Professionals seeking to understand the inner workings of recommendation algorithms will find this subchapter invaluable in their quest to harness the power of AI for personalization.

Recommendation algorithms play a crucial role in enhancing user engagement and satisfaction by offering personalized recommendations that resonate with individual preferences. Through the analysis of user behavior and preferences, AI algorithms can predict and suggest content or services that are most likely to captivate and retain the user's interest. Whether it's recommending a movie on a streaming platform or suggesting a product on an ecommerce site, recommendation algorithms are the driving force behind personalized user experiences that keep users coming back for more.

In the realm of personalized healthcare, recommendation algorithms are revolutionizing the way medical treatments and healthcare services are tailored to individual patient needs and preferences. By leveraging

AI technology, healthcare providers can analyze vast amounts of data to recommend personalized treatment plans that optimize patient outcomes. From suggesting the most effective medication to predicting potential health risks, recommendation algorithms are reshaping the healthcare landscape by putting personalized care at the forefront of patient-centric practices.

In the field of personalized education, recommendation algorithms are being implemented to create tailored learning experiences for students based on their unique learning styles and abilities. By analyzing student performance data and behavior patterns, AI algorithms can recommend personalized educational resources, assignments, and assessments that cater to individual strengths and weaknesses. This personalized approach to education not only enhances student engagement but also fosters a deeper understanding and retention of knowledge, ultimately leading to improved academic outcomes.

As professionals in the AI for Personalization niche, it is essential to understand the significance of recommendation algorithms in various sectors, from healthcare to education. By delving into the intricacies of developing recommendation algorithms, professionals can unlock the full potential of AI technology to create highly personalized user experiences that cater to individual preferences and needs. This subchapter serves as a comprehensive guide for professionals looking to harness the power of recommendation algorithms in their quest to enhance user engagement and satisfaction across industries.

Data Privacy and Security Considerations

Data privacy and security considerations are of utmost importance when it comes to implementing AI for personalization across various industries. As professionals looking to harness the power of AI for personalized user experiences, it is crucial to understand the risks and take proactive measures to protect user data and ensure data security.

In the realm of AI for personalization, user data is often collected and utilized to tailor content and services to individual preferences. This data can include personal information such as browsing history, purchase behavior, and demographic details. It is essential to adhere to strict data privacy regulations and guidelines to safeguard user information and prevent any unauthorized access or misuse of data.

Moreover, as AI algorithms become increasingly sophisticated in their ability to analyze and predict user behavior, there is a growing concern about data security. Hackers and cybercriminals may target AI systems to steal sensitive user data or manipulate algorithms for malicious purposes. Therefore, implementing robust security measures such as encryption, access controls, and regular security audits is essential to protect user data from potential threats.

In the context of AI for personalized healthcare, where sensitive medical information is involved, the stakes are even higher. Healthcare providers must ensure that patient data is securely stored and only accessed by authorized personnel. Additionally, strict data privacy regulations such as HIPAA must be followed to protect patient confidentiality and prevent data breaches.

Overall, as professionals in the field of AI for personalization, it is our responsibility to prioritize data privacy and security considerations in all our endeavors. By implementing best practices in data protection and security, we can build trust with users, comply with regulations, and mitigate the risks associated with AI-powered personalized experiences.

Challenges and Limitations of Personalized AI

One of the main challenges and limitations of personalized AI is the issue of data privacy and security. As AI systems collect and analyze vast amounts of personal data to tailor experiences to individual users, there is a growing concern about how this data is being used and protected. With the increasing number of data breaches and privacy scandals, users are becoming more wary of sharing their personal information with AI systems, which can hinder the effectiveness of personalized experiences.

Another challenge of personalized AI is the potential for bias in algorithms. AI systems are only as good as the data they are trained on, and if this data is biased or incomplete, it can lead to inaccurate or unfair personalized recommendations. For example, in personalized healthcare, biased algorithms could result in certain groups of patients receiving subpar treatment or being excluded from certain medical services based on factors such as race or socioeconomic status. It is crucial for developers to address and mitigate bias in AI algorithms to ensure fair and equitable personalized experiences for all users.

Furthermore, the scalability of personalized AI can be a limitation in certain industries. While AI has the potential to deliver highly personalized experiences at scale, it can be challenging to implement and maintain personalized systems across large user bases. In sectors like personalized healthcare or personalized finance, where individual needs and preferences vary widely, scaling AI systems to accommodate the diverse needs of a large number of users can be a complex and resource-intensive process.

Additionally, the lack of transparency in AI algorithms can pose a challenge for both developers and users. Many AI systems operate as "black boxes," meaning that users do not have insight into how personalized recommendations are being generated. This lack of transparency can lead to distrust and skepticism among users, who may be hesitant to fully engage with personalized AI systems if they do not understand how they work. It is important for developers to prioritize transparency and explainability in AI algorithms to build trust and confidence among users.

Finally, the ethical implications of personalized AI must be carefully considered. As AI systems become more adept at predicting and influencing user behavior, questions arise about the ethical implications of using personalized AI for purposes such as targeted marketing or personalized education. Developers must adhere to ethical guidelines and regulations to ensure that personalized AI is used responsibly and ethically, taking into account issues such as user consent, autonomy, and fairness in decision-making processes. By addressing these challenges and limitations, developers can harness the power of personalized AI to enhance user experiences across industries while upholding ethical standards and protecting user privacy and security.

Chapter 4: Case Studies and Success Stories

Personalized AI in Action: Case Studies from Various Industries

In the subchapter "Personalized AI in Action: Case Studies from Various Industries," we will explore how AI is revolutionizing user experiences in different sectors. From entertainment to ecommerce, AI is driving highly personalized interactions through sophisticated recommendation algorithms. By tailoring content and services to individual preferences, businesses are able to enhance user engagement and satisfaction. Through real-world case studies, professionals will gain valuable insights into the power of personalized AI in delivering exceptional user experiences.

One industry where AI is making a significant impact is healthcare. AI for Personalized Healthcare is being used to tailor medical treatments and healthcare services to individual patient needs and preferences. By analyzing vast amounts of data, AI algorithms can provide personalized recommendations for treatment plans, medication dosages, and preventive care strategies. This personalized approach to healthcare not only improves patient outcomes but also enhances the overall healthcare experience.

In the education sector, AI for Personalized Education is revolutionizing the way students learn. By leveraging AI technology, educators can create personalized learning experiences for students based on their unique learning styles and abilities. Adaptive learning platforms use AI algorithms to track students' progress, identify areas for improvement, and provide tailored learning materials and exercises. This personalized approach to education is empowering students to reach their full potential and achieve academic success.

In the finance industry, AI for Personalized Finance is transforming the way individuals manage their money. By utilizing AI algorithms, financial institutions can offer personalized financial advice and solutions to clients based on their financial goals and habits. AI-powered financial advisors analyze clients' financial data to provide personalized recommendations for investments, savings strategies, and budgeting techniques. This personalized approach to financial planning helps individuals make informed decisions and achieve their financial goals.

In the travel sector, AI for Personalized Travel is enhancing the travel experience for individuals. By leveraging AI technology, travel companies can recommend personalized travel itineraries, accommodations, and activities based on individual preferences. AI algorithms analyze factors such as travel history, preferences, and budget constraints to create customized travel plans that cater to each traveler's unique needs. This personalized approach to travel planning is revolutionizing the way people explore the world and create memorable experiences.

Success Stories of Companies Implementing Personalized AI

In the rapidly evolving landscape of personalized AI, many companies have successfully implemented AI technology to enhance user experiences across various industries. These success stories serve as an inspiration for professionals looking to learn more about the potential of AI for personalization.

One notable success story comes from a leading ecommerce platform that leveraged AI-powered recommendation algorithms to tailor product suggestions to individual customer preferences. By analyzing user behavior and purchase history, the platform was able to significantly increase user engagement and satisfaction, leading to a substantial boost in sales.

In the healthcare sector, a pioneering medical institution implemented AI technology to personalize treatment plans for patients based on their unique needs and preferences. By analyzing medical data and patient feedback, the institution was able to improve patient outcomes and satisfaction levels, demonstrating the power of AI in revolutionizing personalized healthcare services.

Another inspiring success story comes from a prominent online education platform that utilized AI technology to create personalized learning experiences for students. By analyzing student performance data and learning styles, the platform was able to offer tailored lessons and resources, resulting in improved student engagement and academic success.

In the financial sector, a forward-thinking investment firm implemented AI algorithms to provide personalized financial advice and solutions to clients. By analyzing client financial goals and habits, the firm was able to offer customized investment strategies, leading to higher client satisfaction and retention rates.

These success stories underscore the transformative impact of AI for personalization across industries, from healthcare to education to finance. By harnessing the power of AI technology, companies can create highly personalized user experiences that drive engagement, satisfaction, and ultimately, business success.

Lessons Learned and Best Practices

In the subchapter "Lessons Learned and Best Practices", professionals in the field of AI for Personalization can glean valuable insights from various industries where AI is driving highly personalized user experiences. One key lesson learned is the importance of sophisticated recommendation algorithms in tailoring content and services to individual preferences. By understanding user behavior and preferences, businesses can enhance user engagement and satisfaction, ultimately leading to increased customer loyalty and revenue.

Another best practice that professionals can take away from the book "Personalized AI: Enhancing User Experiences Across Industries" is the application of AI for Personalized Healthcare. By using AI to tailor medical treatments and healthcare services to individual patient needs and preferences, healthcare providers can improve patient outcomes and satisfaction. This lesson highlights the potential of AI to revolutionize personalized healthcare and bring about significant advancements in the field.

Furthermore, the subchapter delves into AI for Personalized Education, showcasing how AI technology can create personalized learning experiences for students based on their unique learning styles and abilities. This best practice emphasizes the importance of catering to individual student needs in order to optimize learning outcomes and promote academic success. By implementing AI in education, educators can better support student growth and development.

In addition, professionals can gain insights into AI for Personalized Finance, which utilizes AI algorithms to offer personalized financial advice and solutions to individuals based on their financial goals and habits. This lesson underscores the power of AI in helping individuals make informed financial decisions and achieve their financial objectives. By leveraging AI technology in finance, businesses can enhance customer satisfaction and loyalty while driving business growth.

Overall, the subchapter "Lessons Learned and Best Practices" provides professionals with a comprehensive overview of the various applications of AI for Personalization across industries. By understanding the key lessons and best practices highlighted in the book, professionals can harness the power of AI to create highly personalized user experiences and drive innovation in their respective fields. This subchapter serves as a valuable resource for professionals seeking to learn more about AI for Personalization and its potential impact on various industries.

Chapter 5: The Future of Personalized AI

Emerging Trends in Personalized AI

The field of personalized AI is rapidly evolving, with emerging trends that are shaping the way industries cater to individual preferences and needs. From healthcare to finance, education to fashion, personalized AI is revolutionizing the way services and products are delivered to consumers. In this subchapter, we will explore some of the key emerging trends in personalized AI that are driving enhanced user experiences across various sectors.

One of the most prominent trends in personalized AI is the use of sophisticated recommendation algorithms to tailor content and services to individual preferences. This trend is evident in industries such as entertainment, ecommerce, and gaming, where AI is being used to create personalized experiences that keep users engaged and satisfied. By analyzing user data and behavior, AI algorithms can predict and recommend content that is most likely to resonate with each individual, leading to increased customer satisfaction and loyalty.

Another emerging trend in personalized AI is the use of AI technology in healthcare to tailor medical treatments and services to individual patient needs and preferences. This trend is revolutionizing the way healthcare is delivered, allowing for more personalized and effective treatments that take into account each patient's unique health profile. By leveraging AI algorithms to analyze patient data and medical history, healthcare providers can offer targeted and personalized care that improves patient outcomes and satisfaction.

In the education sector, AI is being used to create personalized learning experiences for students based on their unique learning styles and abilities. This trend is transforming the way students engage with educational content, allowing for more personalized and effective learning experiences that cater to individual needs. By analyzing student data and performance, AI algorithms can recommend and deliver content that is tailored to each student's strengths and weaknesses, leading to improved academic outcomes and student engagement.

In the finance industry, AI is being utilized to offer personalized financial advice and solutions to individuals based on their financial goals and habits. This trend is revolutionizing the way people manage their finances, allowing for more personalized and effective financial planning that takes into account each individual's unique financial situation. By analyzing user data and spending habits, AI algorithms can recommend and implement financial strategies that help individuals achieve their financial goals and objectives.

Overall, the emerging trends in personalized AI are driving highly personalized user experiences across various industries, from healthcare to finance, education to gaming. By leveraging AI technology to create tailored and customized experiences for individuals, businesses and organizations can enhance user engagement, satisfaction, and loyalty, ultimately leading to improved outcomes and success in the marketplace. For professionals looking to stay ahead of the curve and learn more about the potential of AI for personalization, understanding these emerging trends is essential for leveraging the power of personalized AI in their respective industries.

Ethical and Social Implications of Personalized AI

The integration of personalized AI into various industries has opened up new possibilities for enhancing user experiences and satisfaction. As AI technology continues to advance, it is becoming increasingly important for professionals to consider the ethical and social implications of implementing personalized AI systems. These systems have the potential to greatly impact individuals' lives, and it is crucial to ensure that they are used in a responsible and ethical manner.

In the realm of personalized healthcare, AI is being used to tailor medical treatments and healthcare services to individual patient needs and preferences. While this has the potential to greatly improve patient outcomes, it also raises ethical concerns surrounding data privacy and the potential for bias in treatment recommendations. Professionals in the healthcare industry must carefully consider these implications and work to ensure that personalized AI systems are used in a way that prioritizes patient well-being and autonomy.

Similarly, in personalized education, AI technology is being used to create tailored learning experiences for students based on their unique abilities and learning styles. While this has the potential to greatly improve educational outcomes, there are ethical concerns surrounding data privacy and the potential for exacerbating educational inequalities. Professionals in the education sector must carefully consider these implications and work to ensure that personalized AI systems are used in a way that promotes equal access to quality education for all students.

In the realm of personalized finance, AI algorithms are being used to offer personalized financial advice and solutions to individuals based on their financial goals and habits. While this has the potential to greatly improve financial literacy and decision-making, there are ethical concerns surrounding data privacy and the potential for exploitation of vulnerable individuals. Professionals in the finance industry must carefully consider these implications and work to ensure that personalized AI systems are used in a way that prioritizes transparency and consumer protection.

Overall, as personalized AI continues to revolutionize various industries, it is crucial for professionals to consider the ethical and social implications of implementing these systems. By approaching the development and implementation of personalized AI with a strong ethical framework, professionals can ensure that these systems are used in a way that prioritizes user well-being and autonomy, while also promoting social good and equality.

Opportunities for Innovation and Growth

In the realm of AI for Personalization, there are endless opportunities for innovation and growth across various industries. From entertainment to ecommerce, AI is driving highly personalized user experiences that are reshaping the way businesses connect with their customers. By utilizing sophisticated recommendation algorithms, companies are able to tailor content and services to individual preferences, ultimately enhancing user engagement and satisfaction.

One niche where AI is making a significant impact is in the realm of Personalized Healthcare. By leveraging AI technology, medical professionals are able to tailor treatments and healthcare services to meet the unique needs and preferences of individual patients. This not only improves patient outcomes but also enhances the overall healthcare experience.

Similarly, in the field of Personalized Education, AI is revolutionizing the way students learn by creating personalized learning experiences based on their unique learning styles and abilities. This personalized approach to education not only improves student engagement but also helps to unlock their full potential.

In the realm of Personalized Finance, AI algorithms are being used to offer personalized financial advice and solutions to individuals based on their financial goals and habits. This level of customization not only helps individuals make more informed financial decisions but also enhances their overall financial well-being.

Overall, the opportunities for innovation and growth in the realm of AI for Personalization are vast and diverse. Whether it's in the realms of healthcare, education, finance, travel, fitness, fashion, marketing, gaming, home automation, or customer service, AI technology is revolutionizing the way businesses connect with their customers and deliver highly personalized experiences. Professionals looking to stay ahead of the curve in their respective industries would be wise to explore the possibilities that AI for Personalization has to offer.

Chapter 6: Conclusion

Recap of Key Points

In this subchapter, we will recap some of the key points discussed throughout the book "Personalized AI: Enhancing User Experiences Across Industries". We have explored the impact of AI on various sectors, from entertainment to ecommerce, and how sophisticated recommendation algorithms are being used to tailor content and services to individual preferences. This has led to enhanced user engagement and satisfaction in these industries.

One of the key areas we have delved into is AI for Personalized Healthcare. By using AI to tailor medical treatments and healthcare services to individual patient needs and preferences, we are seeing significant advancements in the field. This personalized approach to healthcare is revolutionizing the way medical professionals provide care and is leading to better patient outcomes.

Another important niche we have discussed is AI for Personalized Education. By implementing AI technology to create personalized learning experiences for students based on their unique learning styles and abilities, we are seeing improvements in student engagement and academic performance. This tailored approach to education is helping to meet the individual needs of students and enhance their learning experience.

In the realm of AI for Personalized Finance, we have explored how AI algorithms are being used to offer personalized financial advice and solutions to individuals based on their financial goals and habits. This personalized approach to financial services is helping individuals make better decisions about their money and achieve their financial goals more effectively.

Overall, the use of AI for personalization is transforming various industries and enhancing user experiences across the board. Whether it be in healthcare, education, finance, travel, fitness, fashion, marketing, gaming, home automation, or customer service, AI is playing a crucial role in delivering personalized experiences that cater to individual preferences and needs. As professionals looking to learn more about AI for personalization, it is important to stay informed about the latest advancements and trends in this rapidly evolving field.

Final Thoughts on the Future of Personalized AI

In conclusion, the future of personalized AI is bright and promising for professionals looking to enhance user experiences across various industries. The use of sophisticated recommendation algorithms in AI for personalization is revolutionizing the way content and services are tailored to individual preferences, leading to increased user engagement and satisfaction. From entertainment to ecommerce, AI is driving highly personalized user experiences that are reshaping the way businesses interact with their customers.

Furthermore, AI for personalized healthcare is transforming the medical industry by tailoring treatments and services to individual patient needs and preferences. This personalized approach to healthcare is revolutionizing the way medical professionals deliver care, leading to improved patient outcomes and satisfaction. AI for personalized education is also making waves in the education sector by creating personalized learning experiences for students based on their unique learning styles and abilities, ultimately leading to better academic performance and engagement.

In addition, AI for personalized finance is changing the way individuals manage their finances by offering personalized financial advice and solutions based on their financial goals and habits. This personalized approach to finance is empowering individuals to make better financial decisions and achieve their financial goals. AI for personalized travel, fitness, fashion, marketing, gaming, home automation, and customer service are also revolutionizing their respective industries by offering personalized experiences and services tailored to individual preferences and needs.

Overall, the future of personalized AI is limitless, with endless possibilities for professionals to enhance user experiences and drive innovation across various sectors. By harnessing the power of AI algorithms and technology, businesses can create highly personalized experiences that meet the unique needs and preferences of their customers, ultimately leading to increased engagement, satisfaction, and success in today's competitive market.